LEVEL UP

Bobby E. Stapleton Jr.

Book Layout © 2018 BookDesignTemplates.com

Level Up/ Bobby E. Stapleton, Jr. -- 1st ed.
ISBN 978-1718869004

Dedication

To My Daughters,

Shekinah, Nisya, and Aubree Stapleton, this book is dedicated to you. Just as you do for your dad, this book will do for others. My world wouldn't be complete without you. You are the sunshine that brightens up my life daily. This book will brighten someone's day, just as you three have illuminated my life. I love you guys.

Special Thanks to Cathy Caballero. You are a life saver. Thank you for all that you have done to make this book come to past.

Shirley Hopkins, I thank you. You didn't allow me the chance to sleep on my gift, so I thank you for pushing me to the next dimension of my life.

To the greatest Church, REHOBOTH International Ministries, better known as RIM, I love all of you. You are the best church ever. Thank you all for everything that you do to make ministry easy.

There is more in you than what you can see! According to the Urban Dictionary, when a player of a videogame has earned enough experience points to acquire a new level in a skill or skills, they are said to "level up". Often, this is accompanied by the ability to wield new weaponry, access new places, or begin new assignments. You are about to level up!

The God that we serve is a God of dimensions and levels. Paul reminds us in Romans 1:17, that God's righteousness is revealed from faith to faith. With God, you don't remain on the same level of faith you were on last season. You level up. God has new skills. God has new assignments. God has new places. God has new relationships. God has new purposes. But they are found at the next level. Your ex is in your next!

There are books that give us information. Then, there are books that give us inspiration. However, very few falls into the last category; these books give us information, inspiration, and revelation. I believe in my spirit that God has drawn us to this revelatory book by Bobby E. Stapleton, *Level Up*. Level Up confirms God's progressive work of righteousness, that has the power to move you to your next level. There are more weapons God wants to trust you with! There are new abilities, new character traits, new anointings, new revelations that God has prepared for you. He knows the plans that he has for you. Plans to prosper you and give you an expected end.

Don't settle. To settle, means to accept a set of circumstances in spite of incomplete satisfaction. The reason you are reading this book is because you are not satisfied in some areas of your life. You know that there is more that God has in store for you. You have felt it at other times, but maybe the season and circumstances were not in your favor. But this is your time to level up. As you read this book, allow each thought, truth, nugget, principle, and revelation to permeate each aspect of your life. Be open to the new experience. You are overdue for your breakthrough. Say yes to His will, and yes to His way. And to God be the glory for what He has done through Pastor Stapleton. Be blessed!

Pastor Stanley James

Table of Contents

• D E V O T I O N 1 •

Leading While Bleeding

For to this you have been called, because Christ also suffered for you, leaving you an example, so that you might follow in his steps. He committed no sin, neither was deceit found in his mouth. When he was reviled, he did not revile in return; when he suffered, he did not threaten, but continued entrusting himself to him who judges justly. He himself bore our sins in his body on the tree, that we might die to sin and live to righteousness. By his wounds, you have been healed. {1 Peter 2:21-24}

Have you ever walked and not heard God's voice? Have you ever walked although you don't understand or know the will of God? What do you do when you pray, and God says nothing? Many Pastors and leaders alike know what it means to be tired, frustrated, and wounded. While trying to find grace and understanding, we are often bound by the tribulation of life, and public leadership can be difficult at times.

While being in the public spot light, you are faced with more demands. In ministry, you will get hurt, get tired, and feel like you are standing alone. Often, you will find yourself doing the most for people, and the same people you bend over backwards for, will walk away from you. Through betrayal and loneliness, you must keep walking.

Often, we question God when we are demanded to swallow our pride. God says, your way is not My way, your plans are not My plans, I knew you before the beginning of time. Even when it's hard and we want to give up and question God, we must trust His plan.

We must remember that the enemy may see a blood trail, but the enemy won't find you dead. (If you were at church, I would tell you to look at your neighbor and say, "Neighbor, the enemy won't find me dead.")

The Lord said, "I will make you a steel wall." People will lie to you and shoot you, but you won't feel a thing. The word teaches us, "Be not weary in well doing, for in due season we shall reap if we faint not." If people didn't need me as a Pastor, I would walk away from ministry. However, it is difficult for me to walk away from something in which I never placed myself in the first place. When you are a leader, your job is never done. When you begin doing what you want to do, God will begin to talk to you. What we are called to, we can walk away from, but the CALL shall remain forever. God has placed so much on the inside of us, that if we do not obey his will, everything around will begin to frustrate us. It is our time to do what we are called to do. We must stand up and be the man/woman that God has created us to be. This is not our place of destiny. We must keep walking. We must obey his will and walk into our destiny. *"Though he slay me, yet will I trust in him."* (Job 13:15)

Father, today I choose to follow Your plan for my life. I choose to walk into my destiny. Allow me to see my full potential and allow me to accept my gift and trust Your way. You have placed greatness inside of me; so, help me in all thine ways.
In Jesus name, Amen.

Watch Your Mouth

Have you ever spoke something over your life and it came to pass? Was it something that you prayed and asked God for? Did you stop to think if it would bring joy to your life, or would it bring misery? One thing you must remember in this life, is that you must watch how you speak. Your tongue can bring blessings to your life, as well as curses. *"Death and life are in the power of the tongue, and those who love it shall eat the fruit thereof."* (Proverbs 18:21 KJV) Whether we are speaking spiritually, physically, or emotionally, the tongue still has power.

First, we must realize that God has given us three components: The Access, The Privilege, and The Authority to speak certain things over our life and into the atmosphere. If God has given us so much authority, we must watch how we speak and use the authority that He has given.

What our tongues produce has eternal implication. Our tongues simply reveal what is in our hearts. *"The good man brings good things out of the good stored up in him, and the evil man brings evil things out of the evil stored up in him."* (Matthew 12:35)

As believers, we must speak positive things over our life. We cannot allow toxic people to enter our life and speak negativity. Toxic people will get into our minds, causing their way of thinking to become our own. *"Men must give account on the day of judgement for every careless word they have spoken."* (Matthew 12:36) As Christian believers, we must continue to speak positive, even when we don't see it around us. We should always remember to allow what we speak to bring us to the place where we want to be.

God made us to be expressive beings, and in this world, we are completely lost without communication. As believers, we must continue to honor God with our ways of speaking and conversing. *"I will bless the Lord at all times, his praises shall continually be in my mouth."* (Psalms 34:1)

Father in heaven, I thank You for the gift of life, and for allowing me to worship You. Allow me to speak positively over my life. I choose to place my trust in You. I declare blessings over my life right now. I will forever worship You and praise You. Allow my words to be a blessing to others. Continue to help me encourage everyone that I meet. Lord, I just want to thank You for who You are, and for what You are doing in my life. I bless Your name and I glorify You. I worship You, for You are worthy. In Jesus Name, Amen.

Get It Right Before It's Too Late

Have you ever wondered where you will spend eternity? If you have never thought about that, now is the time. God is on His way back. We are living in our last days, and we all have an appointed time. Have you watched the news on television and wondered, "What is the world coming to?" Tragic things happen so suddenly, that no one knows what tomorrow may bring.

In biblical times, the people wanted to know when the kingdom will come. Jesus disciples asked, *"What will be the sign of your presence?"* (Matthew 24:3) In response to their question, God replied, *"Only Jehovah God knew exactly when the end of this system of things would come."* (Matthew 24:36) However, God did speak on things that would take place before He came to restore the Kingdom.

To seek God's face, we must first get right with Him. Getting it right simply means being the best that you can be right now. Remember, there is no man on the face of this Earth who is living 100% spotless, and God knows that. You are not spotless. Everyone has flaws, and we all mess up in this life.

The word of God tells us that a man falls seven times, yet he gets back up. (Proverbs 24:16) This passage simply tells us that it is never too late to turn your life around. If we have air flowing through our lungs, we can get it right with God.

Morning is coming. I'm not talking about the sunrise of a new day. There will come a time when God will take His children home. God is on His way back. Death is real and taking people every day.

I am reminded of the story, "Death and the Beautiful Lady". In this story, the lady was the most beautiful woman you have ever seen. From the way she wore her hair, to the fancy clothes and jewelry she modeled in. However, as time passed by, her beauty began to fade away. She would see several strands of gray hair, and the more she tried to cover the gray hair, the more they sprouted. One morning, she discovered there were aches and pains in her body. Her body couldn't function to its normal capacity. Awakened by the death angel on her 60th birthday, she tried to inform him that he had not given her a warning beforehand. The death angel reminded her of the gray strands she tried to cover up, and how her body began to change. He said, "These were all signs, but you ignored them. Your beauty was more important to you, which caused you to ignore all the signs given."

Often, we become too caught up in the ways of the world that we ignore the signs from God. We walk in a world that is strange and unknown. Sometimes, we are standing in a crowd and still feel all alone. We question our purpose, our part, and our place on the earth. We are unable to fathom what tomorrow may bring. Now is the time. It is never too late to fix it up with Christ.

Father, I thank You right now for who You are. For I know that we must stand on judgement day. I thank You for the gift of Life. Thank You for keeping our minds and our souls. Father allow us to keep our hearts and minds stayed on You. I stand on Your word knowing that better days are ahead, and victory is on the way. In Jesus Name, Amen.

Father Can You Hold Me Now

Have you ever walked into a store and saw the Footprint portrait? I believe we all have seen this picture. It portrays God holding someone, showing only one set of foot prints in the sand. This simply means: "God got us." That's not the correct English, but it sounds better that way. Even when life throws you disappointments, heartaches, trials, tribulations, doubts and frustrations, we must remember to always keep our eyes fixed on Christ. God will carry you through it all. God allows the enemy to knock us down to get our attention. Once He gets our attention, we can focus on what He has for us. In the scripture, it tells us, *"And let us not be weary in well doing for in due season we shall reap, if we faint not."* (Galatians 6:9)

God has a hedge of protection around us. Even when we fall or stumble, God keeps us covered. Everyone goes through seasons where the challenges of life seem to weigh us down. During these times, it is easy to turn our eyes away from God. Don't become weary and give up, because God wants to do something awesome in your life. God wants you to live. You are not going to die prematurely. You will not die until it is your time to leave here. God wants to do miraculous things in your life. God wants to prove some things to you. He wants to operate some things in your life, and He wants to minister some things to you. He has you just where He wants you. This is not your place of destiny, but He wants to take you to higher heights. It is your time to live. God has built a wall of protection all around you. Do not get caught up in situations that you do not belong in. Do not get head over heels in lustful situations. There is so much more God wants from you. You shall live and not die.

When it seems like your world has crumbled, remember what God has done for you. Remember when you were falling, and God picked you up. Think back to when you were drowning, and God jumped in and threw you a life line. Today, I want to encourage you to walk in kingdom authority. I want you to walk with your head held high for our God said, *"I will be with you until the end of the world."* (Matthew 28:20) The enemy comes to kill, steal, and destroy, but remember, no matter what the enemy throws your way, God has you. If God is for you, then who can be against you.

Father, thank You for favor. Thank You for turning things around even when I didn't see a way. Lord, I thank You for working things out for my good. Lord, thank You for carrying me and keeping me safe in Your arms. Father through Your word, I shall live and not die. I shall continue to look to the hills from which all my help comes from. My help comes from You. Thank You for preparing a path of victory. Father allow me to keep my eyes on You. In Jesus Name, Amen.

Making Time for What You Love (Part I)

"For God so loved the world that He gave his only begotten Son that whosoever believes in Him shall not perish, but have everlasting life."
(John 3:16)

Are you making time for what you love? You may be wondering to yourself, "Well of course I make time for what I love. I help my children with their homework, and I take them anywhere they want to go on weekends. I come home from work, and I cook dinner. I even have movie night with my significant other." Yet, how often are you making time for GOD? As people, and as Christians, we say we love God, but how much time do we spend with Him?

Matthew 6:24 reads, *"No one can serve two masters, for either he will hate one and love the other, or he will be devoted to one and despise the other."* Living in a world where everything takes money, we become dependent on our jobs. We spend endless nights in the office trying to complete a project, or we go to our boss requesting overtime. We not only abandon our family for the love of money, but we abandon God as well. The word of God teaches us in Matthew 6:33, *"But first seek ye the kingdom of Heaven and his righteousness and all these things will be added to you."*

If we put God back into the equation, money will always be more than what we can handle. Our blessings could be pouring out, but we took God out the equation, and we refuse to spend time with Him. The scripture tells us that God so loved the world. It didn't just say that He loved the world, it stated that He "SO LOVED" the world that He gave His only son to come down from heaven and die for us, so that we may have eternal life with Him in heaven. God made time for us. He loved us so much, that He sacrificed His one and only child (Christ) just for us. Ask yourself, how much of my time am I going to give to God.

"But when you pray, go into your room and shut the door and pray to your Father who is in secret, and your Father will see in secret and he shall reward you." (Matthew 6:6) What does your prayer life look like? Prayer is our one on one time to speak with the Almighty Creator. God doesn't ask much of us, yet we turn our backs on Him. When our back is up against the wall and we want God to come through, we automatically become available for God. He wants us to make time for Him. There are three things we must remember:

1) If you love something or someone- {You make time for them}

2) If you love something or someone- {You provide for them}
3) If you love something or someone- {You protect them}

Now, let's look back at the scripture listed above in John 3:16. Allow me to break it down for you:
1) For God so loved the world = {He made time for us}
2) He gave his only begotten son = {He provided} The only way to Him is through His SON. {He made a way}
3) We shall not perish= {Protected Us} Through Christ and Salvation, we shall not die but live eternally with Christ in heaven.

God made time for us, therefore, it is up to us to make time for Him. How will you spend your time? Your time spent today will determine how your time will be spent in eternity.

Father in heaven, we thank You for loving us so much that You sacrificed Your only Son, so that we may spend our eternity in Heaven with You. We just praise You Father for the gift of life. We ask that You continue to build a wall of protection around us and continue to keep us covered in Your blood. We will forever give You the glory, and the honor for You are so worthy. In your son Jesus name, Amen.

Attitude Is Everything

How grateful are you? If I asked you to make a list of everything you were grateful for, would it be shorter than everything you complain about? When was the last time you praised God for His gratefulness or even lifted your hands to tell Him thank you? It took you a moment to think back didn't it? We all allow our attitudes to get the best of us sometimes.

James 4:10 reads, *"Humble yourselves before the Lord, and He will lift you up."* Having a grateful attitude will surpass what we are going through. When God sent His only Son down to the Earth, He displayed a positive attitude. As believers of God, we should be grateful for the effort and sacrifices that God made just for us.

At this moment in our lives, we must stop complaining and be grateful for where we are. We can impact so many lives just by having a positive attitude. A positive attitude is everything. *"Do everything without grumbling or arguing."* (Philippians 2:14)

Sharing a kind word, giving a hug, or showing a beautiful smile will turn someone's darkest day into a beautiful, sunshine filled day. Displaying a grateful attitude can help save a life. Displaying a positive attitude can also bring a lost soul to Christ. Our actions and the way we carry ourselves speak volumes. As

Christians, we are often looked upon as examples. So, this means we must make sure that our attitude is positive.

When you look in the mirror what does your attitude say about you? Will you continue going through life complaining, or will you begin to speak positivity over your life? When things go wrong, learn how to praise Him. When you are sick in your body, praise Him. When your bank account is empty, praise Him. When you have lost your job and you cannot make ends meet, praise Him. We must learn how to praise Him in every aspect of our lives. When Jesus died upon the cross, He never said a mumbling word. He stretched out His arms, lowered His head and He died. As Jesus hung on the cross, He still gave His Father praise. We must be like Christ, and possess a positive and grateful attitude.

Lord, thank You for who You are. Thank You for loving me even when I was too selfish and ungrateful to love myself. Lord, thank You for blessing me despite my ungratefulness. Lord allow me to be a vessel to someone who maybe standing in need of Your presence. Allow my positive and grateful attitude to take me to the next level in life. I give You honor and glory for who You are. You are worthy to be praised. In Jesus Name, Amen.

Making Time for What You Love (Part II)

"For God so loved the world that He gave His only begotten Son that whosoever believes in Him shall not perish but have everlasting life."
{John 3:16}

How much time are you making for the things and people you love? This topic is so important, I decided to do a part two.

Have you ever had a favorite singer who was coming to a city near you? As the date became closer, you made sure that everything was taken care of. Your clothes were already picked out and your car was clean. We as people will make time for irrelevant people and things. However, we won't spend any time with the creator who gave us life.

Love REQUIRES time. God wants our undivided attention and our time. The more we pour into God, the more He will pour into our lives. How can we say we love our creator if we are not doing the following:

- Opening His Word and reading it, meditating on it , and obeying it.

- Praying (One on One time with God)
- Attending Church

Every opportunity we must show our love for God, we become too busy or preoccupied. As believers of God, we should never become too content with where we are with God. Ask yourself, do I really love God or am I lusting after God? As humans, we want God to do so many wonderful things for us, but we can't even tell Him thank you. God sits high and looks low. He sits in the most comfortable place in the world, Heaven. God made time for His children. God sacrificed His one and only son to come down from Heaven to Earth because God knew we needed His son to help us, bless us, cover us, mold us, restore us, and guide us. God was not inconvenienced. He became available because He loved us so much. When Jesus left Earth, He told His disciples that He would send a comforter (The Holy Spirit). The Holy Spirit is our comforter, our counselor, and He is standing by knocking on the doors of our heart.

When you love something, you change your way of thinking. The love of God will make you change your habits and your passion. Once we are saved, we become content with the way things are going in our lives, and the enemy begins to plan His attack. The enemy will send something or someone in your life as a distraction, whether it is an old flame, a job that will consume your time (so you think), or an old friend who partied with you. The enemy sends you notifications. You stop attending church, praying and fasting. Now you have been going through, you're at death's door, and all the odds are stacked against you. However, God steps in and makes a way every single time.

We apologize to God, and we ask Him to come back into our lives because we want to get this thing right. God is so much bigger than just a shout. Christianity has become more about religion, than developing a relationship with Christ. We allow the enemy to come in and kill us softly. As Christian believers, God does not ask for much. We must start to align our lives with Christ. To get closer to God and make time for the creator of life, we must first:

•Start (Even if you start small: reading one scripture per day, praying 10 minutes instead of 30 minutes, attending mid-week service or Sunday School)

•Start saying NO (Other people's responsibilities should not become your priority due to their lack of responsibility.) Stop allowing other people's problems to take your eyes from GOD. Create boundaries for yourself.

•Waking up 30 minutes early (This should be time spent with God, praying and reading His word.)

When we refuse to spend time with God and do His will, we are slapping God in the face. We are disrespecting the man who gave the life of His Son for us. If we love God, we must show God we love Him. We must make sacrifices. Freedom from distractions, sin, and our desires frees us to please God by doing, and being, the best that we can before Him.

Father, I thank You for Your Holy Spirit who has been my comforter, my protector, and helper, in this life. Father, I thank You for the gift of life and for sacrificing Your one and only son. Lord, become convenient for me so that I may live eternal life in Heaven with You. Father help me on this journey as I spend more time in Your presence and I show my love for You. Thank You for loving me so unconditionally. Even when I was unworthy, you loved me through it all. Thank You for not treating me as my sins deserve. I honor and love You the rest of my days. In Jesus Name, Amen.

Behind the Scene

"Have I not commanded you? Be strong and courageous.
Do not be frightened, and do not be dismayed, for the Lord your
God is with you wherever you go."
(Joshua 1:9)

Have the curtains closed in your life? If your answer is YES, remember in Psalms, David said, "The Lord is my strength and my shield; in Him my heart trusts, and I am helped; my heart exults and my song I give thanks to Him." {Psalms 28:7}

Although the curtain has closed in your life, the production is not over. The moment you're ready to quit is usually the moment right before a miracle happens.

While the curtains are closed, God is only rearranging somethings in our lives. "But as it is written, eye hath no seen, nor ear heard, neither have enter the heart of man, the things which God hath prepared for them that love him." (1 Corinthians 2:9) God has placed you in hiding simply by the closing of the curtains. Viewers are praying that you will not succeed. They prejudge without even knowing your circumstances, and often they become a distraction. There are times when we want to just throw in the towel. We cry, we say we are tired, and we walk out, but get ready because your miracle is on the way.

God is shielding us, molding us, equipping us, and strengthening us for our miracle. Our greater is coming. When I think of the closed curtain, I am reminded of the Inspirational Poem, "Don't Quit." At the very end of the poem the author states, "So stick to the fight when you're hardest hit - It's when things seem worst that you must not quit."

Our closed curtain teaches us to keep pushing, to keep trusting in His will, and to appreciate our open curtains. The production is not over, greater is coming.

Father, thank You for protecting me. Thank You for the closed curtains in our lives. Father, all our help comes from You. In trying times, we must keep our hands in Your hands and our eyes on You. Father thank You for scene one. Lord, help prepare me for my final encore. Continue to protect me behind the scenes. In Jesus name, Amen.

Should Not Perish
{Protect What You Love}

For God so loved the world, He gave His only begotten Son that whosoever believeth in Him shall not perish but have everlasting life."
{John 3:16}

How many of us can say that we have seen the face of the almighty Holy One? Although, we may not have seen His face, we have heard His voice. If we have never seen His face, how do we know God is real? We know that God is real, because of our faith in Him. It is impossible to please our Father (God) if there is no faith.

As believers, we must walk in the spirit of God. We are ambassadors for Christ. You may not have seen His face, but people see your face daily. What do people see in you? Are you saved on Sunday morning, and cursing people out on Sunday evening? If we love God, we must portray Christianity to others. How can we say we love God, whom we have never seen, but hate our brother and sister whom we see daily?

Protecting God at all cost consist of living a lifestyle per His will. We are in the world, but not of the world. The only time we should be of the world is when we are preaching and sharing the gospel with others. You must protect your brand (GOD). If you walk in any Chick-Fil-A restaurant around the world, you are welcomed with great customer service. The staff goes above and beyond to display excellence. The CEO of the company is pleased. His brand is being protected. His staff reflects him. God is the CEO of believers. How well is your customer service? How does your attitude affect others? Is God pleased with how you represent His brand? Are you a vibrant and beautiful spirit who greet others with a smile, or are you a demonic spirit who display a nasty attitude? As believers, and as a church, we represent God, but we are doing a poor job.

Lost souls enter a sanctuary and we display judgment. We look down on others. We throw up their past and we turn our backs. God is a God of love; therefore, we should display love. But, how are we showing Him? If we love God, we should protect Him.

In the scripture John 3:16, God displayed love and protected us. It shows the conditions of this world. God left His comfortable place in heaven and came to Earth swaddled in a blanket and lying in a manger, because comfortable people on Earth were doing uncomfortable things. He came as Jesus to show us the way, due to our wrong doing. Grace and mercy cover our wrong doing so that we may see Heaven. We all have sinned and fallen short of God's glory, but grace and mercy keep us and protects us. God protected what He loved. As

Christians and believers of God, we must protect our brand. We must protect God by continuing to live a lifestyle pleasing to Him.

Dear Heavenly Father, I just want to thank You. Thank You for being the God that You are. Thank You for You protecting us. Thank You for loving us unconditionally. Thank You for displaying Your love to us. I pray that we can become more and more like You each day Father. In Jesus name, Amen.

Don't Stop, Get It, Get It

"But as for you, be strong and don't give up, for your work will be rewarded"
2 Chronicles 15:7

When you feel like giving up, you are missing out on what our Father in Heaven must offer. In our lives, there will be many things that will require our attention, but remember it is very important to stay on course and never give up. Isaiah 41:10 states, *"So do not fear, for I am with you; do not be dismayed, for I am your God. I will strengthen you and help you; I will uphold you with my righteous right hand."*

There will be things that will try to stop you or deter you from your assignment. The enemy comes to steal, kill, and destroy. Our Lord and Savior tell us, *"The race is not given to the swift, nor the battle to the strong, ... but he who endures until the end."* (Ecclesiastes 9:11)

How will you start? You will begin by placing God as the head. Each day apply those gifts and use them to make it to the finish line. People who start with you, will not end with you.

Everyone in this life is not always meant to go where God is trying to take you. Some people will be left behind. Remember one thing: Jesus chose Judas, but Judas didn't choose Jesus. There will be people who will not understand your journey, but you must not stop your vision. You must keep walking, keep running, leap into your journey, and do not stop. Stopping is not an option. You have come too far to stop and turn around.

Father thank You for the tools and the vision that has been placed upon my life. Father give me the strength to endure. Allow me to climb every mountain and cross every sea. Father continue to have Your way in my life. I thank You for the gift of life. The race is not given to the swift, nor to the battle to the strong, but to the one who endures to the end. Father I ask that You cover me while I continue to run this race. In Jesus Name, Amen.

Provide for What You Love

"For God so loved the world, He gave His only begotten Son that whosoever believeth in Him shall not perish, but have everlasting life"
(John 3:16)

How are you living? Are you living a life of giving? To provide for what you love, you must display a lifestyle of giving. Let us take a moment to look at our lives in two categories: Life as Rock or Life as a Sponge.

Life as a rock	Life as a sponge
• No matter what we pour into it, nothing will ever come out.	• Live a life of peace and comfort.
• No matter how many blessings are being poured in, it will just roll off like water from a duck's back.	• Absorb Everything that is poured in.
• Live a Life of Struggle	
• What we pour in, will pour out.	

Many people live their life as a rock. They pretend to act on faith, but do not believe. To see what God has for us, we must change our way of thinking. We must change our actions to believe and trust GOD. As children of God, we must live the life of a faithful believer, and we must have a heart of a sponge. The more we give to others, the more our Father who sits in Heaven will pour into us.

When God takes things from us, many think it is to hinder us. But in fact, God is making room to bless us for something greater. God gave us the whole world, and He gave it to us by:

•Making time for what He love: For God so loved the world
•Providing for what He love: He gave His only begotten son
•Protecting what He love: We shall not perish (crucifixion) He made a sacrifice so that we may have eternal life with Him in Heaven.

It has been said that the secret to a great life is giving. No matter how busy our lives are or even if we feel unworthy or useless, we all have something to offer. We often miss the opportunity to understand that our life makes a difference. When we begin to give to others around us, it reminds us of what we are made of. It reminds us of who God designed us to be. When we are tired, we find the strength to continue. Now is the time that we must reach within us and find strength to live a life of giving.

Father, thank You for sacrificing Your only son so You may give us a life of eternity with You. If there were no Judas, there would be no cross; and if there were no cross there would be no You and me.

Father, we thank You for the cross. We thank You for the gift of life. Allow us to pour into others as our Father in Heaven open windows and pour into us. In Jesus Name, Amen.

Jumping Off in Life

Where are you in life? Do you feel like you are standing at the crossroad or you are facing a difficult situation? Maybe you are in the middle of a divorce or battling the loss of a job. As Christians, we all face many different adversities in our life. However, we must understand that God will not place more on us than we can bare. If God gave it to you, then He is more than able to take you through it.

No matter what kind of hand you have been dealt in this life, you must know how to play the cards that have been dealt. How many of you have played the game of UNO as a child or even in your adult life? When I think of this game several cards come to mind. As we begin to play the game of UNO, let us glance at the "SKIP" card. Often, we want things so badly that God will skip over us until it is our time. God has not forgotten us. During the skip phase, He is preparing and equipping us for our time. Now, we have the "REVERSE" card. Sometimes, we must go back and gather the information that has already been laid out before us. We forget where God brought us from, and sometimes He has a way of taking us back there. Finally, my favorite card of them all, the "WILD" card. I consider the "WILD" card as GOD's way of placing a ram in the bush. When we feel like giving up and throwing in the towel, God always places the perfect person in our lives at the right time, and He gives us a way out.

You may have lost your job and did not how you were going to make ends meet. Then, God stepped in and granted you with a job making double the salary you had on your previous job. You may have lost your house and out of nowhere God showed up and blessed you with another one. God always places a ram in the bush. He will always throw you a "WILD" card.

God will not leave us on our own. God is not silent, He hears our every cry. He has given us the commandments to help carry us through every obstacle in our lives. As you begin to jump off in life, ask yourself, "What is keeping me from being the best that I can be? Does my family, education, life experiences, fear, lack of obedience, self-control, the flesh, lack of support, or maybe lack of motivation keeping me from being the best I can be?" In these things, you cannot get to the next level if these things are placed in the hands of others.

Do not allow others to dictate your life or your next move. It starts with you, and you must stop making excuses for where you are in life. Start where you are today. Start making your pizza even if you don't have an oven. Stop allowing yourself to be behind time and beneath the era. You must start now. God knows what to give you and how to give it to you. Stop allowing opportunities to slip through your fingers and go after your dreams. *"Therefore, I tell you, do not worry about your life, what you will eat or drink, or about your body, what you will wear. Is not life more important than food, and the body more important that clothes? Look at the birds of the air; they do not sow or reap or store away in barns, and yet your heavenly Father feeds them. Are you not much more valuable than they? Who of you by worrying can add a single hour to his life? And why do you worry about clothes? See how the lilies of the field grow. They do not labor or spin. Yet, I let you that not even Solomon in all his splendor was dressed like one of these. If that is how God clothes the grass of the field, which is here today, and tomorrow is thrown in the fire, will he not much more clothe you, O you of little faith? So, do not worry, saying, 'What shall we eat? Or what shall we drink? Or what shall we wear?' For the pagans run after all these things, and your heavenly Father knows that you need them. But seek first his kingdom and his righteousness, and all these things will be given to you as well."* (Matthew 6:25-33)

No matter where you are in life, remember God has you and God will take care of His own. You must start right now, right where you are, and if you take two steps then God will guide you the rest of the way.

Father God, once more and again, we thank You for the gift of life. We thank You for where we are right now in our lives. We know if we place our trust in You that You will continue to place a ram in the bush, open doors that were shut in our face, and You will guide us in every aspect of our lives. We give Your name the honor and glory. We magnify You. In Jesus Name, Amen.

You Are Too Close to Your Destiny

"Praise be to the God and Father of our Lord Jesus Christ, the Father of Compassion and the God of all comfort, who comfort us in all our troubles, so that we can comfort those in any trouble with the comfort we ourselves receive from God"
2 Corinthians 1:3-4

How do you know it is time to walk into the destiny God has for you? The most difficult part of finding out your destiny is knowing what to place your focus on. Below are steps to help you understand that you are getting close to reaching your destiny:

• Timing: There may be a certain period in your life where God may seem silent, or you may not hear His voice. God is teaching you how to grow deeper in your spirituality. He is equipping you for a major transition.

• Testing: God will place you in a situation beyond your control to keep your eyes stayed on Him, and to keep you lifted and proactive.

• Attacks from the Enemy: There will be times in your life where you think you are on track and focused, yet the enemy throws you into a hardship or you encounter a storm. In that moment you must find direction and guidance from God.

• The spotlight: Understand that your timing is not in God's plan for your life. Everything will unfold when it is in His will and in His own timing. Your destiny will unfold over time.

As believers and Christians, we are often afraid to move forward because we have a fear of making a mistake or disappointing God. We must get out of these negative patterns and change for the better. To get to the next level, we must change our way of thinking. Stay woke and stay focused, because in God's timing we will reach our destiny.

Dear Heavenly Father, thank You for another chance at life. Thank You for being the amazing God that You are. Lord, help me to understand that I came into this world already a champion; special and unique. I am a miracle predetermined by You. Help me to know that I have a unique destiny, and that my destiny is not the same as my dream. Again, I thank You Lord for keeping me. In Jesus name, Amen.

The Rapture: I Must Get Home

"For we must all appear before the judgement seat of Christ, so that each of us may receive what is due to us for the things done while in the body, whether good or bad."
2 Corinthians 5:10

Wondering about the end times and the rapture can cause confusion, worry, and fear for a lot of people, even Christians! While sitting at home watching television, I stumbled across one very familiar movie. In this movie, there was a young man by the name of Elliott, and he met this friend from outer space. Now, his friend was not a human like you or I, his friend was an extra-terrestrial being. He was someone who was not of this world. While watching the movie in one scene the young boy and the alien were holding a conversation and E.T.'s finger began to light up as he pointed to the sky stating, "E.T. go home! E.T. go home!" We as believers must be like E. T. we must be ready to go home when our name is called.

Jesus is on his way back. *"But about that day or hour no one knows, not even the angel in heaven, nor the Son, but only the Father."* (Mark 13:32) We cannot build success or an empire on Earth because this world is not our home. Just stop and look over what God is showing us. Our time here is not long. We must move and get out of here. God is going to crack the sky, and the dead will rise with Him and the ones left here will be caught up in the sky with

Him. *"And if I go and prepare a place for you, I will come back and take you with me that you also may be where I am."* (John 14: 3)

Make sure your house is in order. We cannot be living this life just to die and go to hell. God has given us the study guide with all the answers. Will we pass or fail the test? We must be like E.T. We must go home. Will you be ready?

Father, I know that I have broken Your laws and my sins have separated me from You. For I am truly sorry, and I want to turn away from my sinful ways. I believe that Your Son, Jesus Christ, died for my sins, and is alive, and hearing my daily prayers. Thank You for sending Your Holy Spirit to help me to obey You and do Your will for the rest of my life. In Jesus name, Amen.

Can You Stand the Rain?

"On a perfect day, I know that I can count on you, when that's not possible, tell me can you weather the storm?"
-New Edition-

Many times, in our life we will go through a storm. As we encounter a storm in our life, we must ask ourselves are we able to withstand the storm? Can we stand the rain? A storm can be chaos, secrets within, lies, or a temporary loss within your marriage, relationship or in your home? When these things arise are you able to pull through?

As I minister to couples who are preparing themselves for marriage, in our counseling sessions this a question that I ask. We are excited when the sun comes and shine so brightly upon us, but we become upset when the rain comes. We can't stand the rain because we are unable to make it work for us.

We must change our mindset from "I hope it doesn't happen" to "in case it happens, I'll be ready." We carry an umbrella inside our cars just in case it rains; we are prepared. We all know we will die, so burial and life insurance is put in motion just for that reason. Therefore, we will be prepared for when that time comes.

God sends the rain to make us humble. Without the rain, we would be weak individuals struggling to get through this thing we call life. We must go through it, to grow through it. It is just one big dressed up storm. Here are three points to help you get through the storm of life:

- Rain makes you grow, and it makes you who you are designed to be. If I had sunshine all my life, I would be weak. I can take what comes my way because I had rain in my life.
- Rain washes away everything that is not attached.
- Rain lowers the temperature of the Earth.

As believers, are you able to withstand the rain? Can you keep a smile on your face when you know you have been talked about? Can you continue to come to church when you know you've been lied on? As believers, we must stop giving up on something that we are prepared for. We are built for this, and we will come out with fire and vengeance. Proverbs 18:10 says, "The name of the Lord is a strong tower, the righteous run into it and are safe." No matter how much rain pours into our lives, through God we can stand it. We can get through it because we are designed for it.

Dear Heavenly Father, You remind us over and over again in Your word that You are always with us. You tell us not to fear and You draw us close in Your presence. You are the only place we find refuge in the storms that surround us right now. You are the only place we find peace and strength. Lord, we ask for Your words of truth and Your power to strengthen us. Thank You for Your goodness, grace and mercy. In Jesus name, Amen.

It's Not Supposed to Hurt Like This

"Many are the afflictions of the righteous, but God will deliver them out of it all"
Psalms 34:19

Frederich Neitzche once said, "What doesn't kill us makes us stronger." We human beings are problem-solving animals. Solving problems for us is like fetching tennis balls for a dog. As you say, it is impossible to live a perfect existence. Life is usually a matter of dealing with one problem after another. Problems teach us problem solving skills, but they also teach us to put things in perspective. Problems also teach us to separate the big stuff from the small stuff. Solving problems also give us the confidence that we can handle most of the stuff that will happen to us each day.

If you think back over your life, you will discover the problems you endured changed your life and made you stronger than ever before. To be stronger, you must go through some things because you are stronger than the storm you are facing. While going through, you must also learn from these life changing events.

You will stumble, and you will trip. However, you must remember broken pieces still float. We will encounter trials and tribulations. But remember, the race is not given to the swift nor the battle to the strong, but to the one who endured until the end.

God created us to be undefeated. It may be raining on the outside, but we must keep walking as we are waiting for the sun to shine because we are stronger than what life throws at us.

Lord I thank You. For You are the God of the impossible. You can do anything but fail. I want to trust in Your ability, and not in my own. Teach me to see the difficulties of life from Your perspective. Help me to focus on You and Your power. I want to be like Joshua and Caleb who believed in a good report and focused on You even in hard circumstances. Help me to not fear, but to trust in You during the good, as well as the bad. I declare my faith in Your ability to fulfill Your promises to me. For You are mighty, powerful, righteous, and true. In Jesus name, Amen.

DEVOTION 17

Getting Out

Have you ever been in a position where you just wanted to get out? You find yourself worrying, crying, and praying to God for help and it seems like He is so distant. There may be several things you want to be released from such as, debt, depression, broken marriages, hopeless relationships, and/or bad job experiences. Romans 13:7 reads, "Pay to all what is owed to them: taxes to whom taxes are owed, revenue to whom revenue is owed, respect to whom respect is owed, honor to whom honor is owed."

We are required to pay back what we borrowed, because we want to keep our promise. No matter what we may endure in this season, we expect God to deliver us and pay on His promise to us. A promise of deliverance, a promise of healing, and surrender. How can we expect God to pay on His promise if we don't obey or trust His will?

Our entire Christian life is built on a promise, including those for eternal life and resurrection. Sometimes, we become disappointed in God because we think He failed to keep His word. The problem is, we fail to understand because we are not faithful. Circumstances happen beyond our control that prevents us from keeping our promise, but God never fails on His promise to us.

God does not treat us as our sin deserves. He forgives us for every past mistake we have made, every evil thought, senseless act, and everything that was unpleasing in His eyesight. God promised that He will deliver us from it all.

God's promises will never return void. If God can keep His promise to us, as believers we must keep our eyes on Him. We must trust in Him, honor Him, and keep our promise to Him. God will bless His children for their faithfulness, dedication, and loyalty to His commandments. Every mess that we place ourselves in, God reaches deep down and grab us out of. Getting out is done by fasting and praying. If we pray and pray, we shall reap if we faint not.

Prince of peace, I find myself unable to cope with life sometimes. Instead of feeling grateful, I feel bogged down by the responsibilities that You've given me. Help me to grow closer to You, Father. Circumstances will rarely be ideal; I know that. But I also know that the only thing that makes life worthwhile is living it with You. For I know that if I spend time with You, things will be better. I will be better. In Jesus name, Amen.

Don't Worry, I'll Get It Back

*"You have no choices about how you lose, but you do have a
choice about how you come back and prepare to win again."*
-Pat Riley-

How do you respond to the statement, "You gotta lose to know how to win?" Life will throw you a curve ball. Life will cause you to expect the unexpected, but no matter what, we must stay the course. You will experience a period in your life when you are losing. Nothing right seems to be happening in your life. You are expecting a drought but remember it won't always be like this. God will, and God can turn it all around in your favor. Our worst season only comes to make us better and stronger than before.

As songwriter Fantasia said, "You gotta lose to win again". Often, a lost is a gain. This means that greater is coming. Let's imagine you prayed for a job and God didn't answer it. We become frustrated, angry, and we even begin to question God. You would consider that a lost. A missed opportunity. However, it is a gain. God allows us to miss out on opportunities to bless us with what He has planned for our life.

Everything we lose in this season, we shall get it back. Consider three tactics when you are on the race for a blessing from God:

- Pursue---Go In!
- Overtake---Take over any situation or obstacle!

- Recover All---Take back what the devil stole!

We will stumble, fall, and often time trip, but we must get back up. We must get back in line. You cannot get to the next level in life on the ground. We must pick ourselves up, dust ourselves off, trust God, and stand firm on His will. A loss is not always a loss, in fact it is a gain. When you are serving God, it will not always be easy. But one thing we all know, it will be worth it in the end.

Dear God, thank You for every door that was shut in my face. Thank You, Lord, for every opportunity that I missed out on. Because when those doors were shut in my face, new doors began to open in my life. Doors of better opportunities, doors of higher callings, doors of divine greatness, and most importantly, doors that led me right down the path that You had planned for me. Thank You, Lord, for just being an unchanging God. In Jesus name, Amen.

Release

"God gives many kinds of special abilities, but it is the same Spirit who is the source of them all. There are different kinds of service to God, but it is the same Lord we are serving. There are many ways in which God works in our lives, but it is the same God who works in and through all of us."

(1 Corinthians 12:4-6)

Have you ever looked deep down within yourself to release your full potential? Can you truly say that you have maximized the full potential that God has placed inside of you? Often, the full capabilities of our potential and talents go hidden within. If you decide that you want to release potential that is locked away inside of you, you must understand God's plan for you.

Ask God to release you from other people's mindsets. They do not think that you can make it, and they do not want to see you get there. The enemy knows how to keep you from being free. As believers, we must remove ourselves from naysayers, witches, and warlocks. Anything and/or anyone that holds you bound and keeps you from being free is a witch. We are so used to being bound that we do not know how it feels to be free. It is important that we must walk in the supernatural and lose ties with people.

Look in the mirror and tell yourself, "I was not created to be average, I was created to be a legend." Where you are, is not your destination. You must transition and stop sleeping on yourself. Asking the Father to deliver us from our ways is His way of preparing us for the next level in life. Lord, please deliver me from people. Pray this daily and watch how God moves in your life. You are no longer bound, you are officially released.

Dear Heavenly Father, thank You for another day's journey. Thank You for being the God of another chance. I pray that You release me from the mindset of others. I pray that You break every chain that is keeping me from reaching my full potential. For I decree that I am no longer bound. Miracles are forming, and blessings are being released all over my life. Thank You Lord for holding my hand and never letting it go. In Jesus name, Amen.

Know Your Judas

"When the enemy comes in like flood, the Spirit of God will raise standard against him!"

Isaiah 59:19

Sometimes living for God is a real battle and a real fight. However, we must understand that even during this battle the enemy can't touch you. We are living in a day and time where we are against one another. You think you have a friend, but that is friend is just your JUDAS. We are supposed to stand for the same thing, and that is the offering of Jesus. (Bringing lost souls to Christ)

As humans, we allow the enemy to attack us, but if God be for us, then who can be against us. When the enemy begins to tempt you, what is the first thing you should do? We must go to God in prayer and we must go to the word of God. The best way to stop an attack is to counter-attack. If you stop entertaining your clown, he will stop performing.

Do you think God knew who Judas was? Of course, He did. He knew Judas would betray Him, just as He knew Peter would deny Him. However, because of Judas, Jesus suffered and went to the cross. Although He suffered, on the third day after His death, He rose. When Jesus got up, He was not the same. He got up with ALL POWER in His hands. He may have died just a young man to some, but He rose a King.

You may be dying in a situation right now because of your Judas. You may be suffering and don't know which way to go, but God is in control and He is going to turn your suffering into a praise. When you rise, you will rise with victory, joy, and love. You will take back everything that Judas tried to take from you. Know your Judas, know your connection, and be aware of wolves in sheep's clothing. Your best defense is an offense!

Lord, I just want to thank You. Thank you for my Judas because without my Judas, I would not be able to rise with victory, joy, and love. Without my Judas, I would not go through my suffering. And Lord, without my suffering I would not have found total peace within You. Thank You for my good days and my bad days. Thank You for my high mountains, and my low valleys. In Jesus name, Amen.

Stay Low

When we face tough times, we become confused, frustrated, and disillusioned. In the book of Psalms, David goes through so much and yet he still trusted and obeyed more than any of us ever could. God has a purpose behind our problems. Choosing to stay low and humble will allow your problems to cease and not get the best of you.

As Christians, sometimes we have certain views and expectations we pick up on by listening to others. We will go through trials, troubles, and tribulations, but what will we do when it happens? What lesson will we learn from it? How do we grow better and not become weary or bitter?

The lower you get; the higher God will rise you. If a person cannot walk with you in your valley, do not let them shine when you are on your mountain. Everything you do in your life is for the glory of God. You will not be able to move up in life if your past is still attached to you. When God tests us, or even when we are faced with troubles, we must remain low. We need to see it as a moment for us to solely trust His will and plans for our life. By trusting Him when we are low and humble, God will move mountains. He will open doors that was once shut in our faces. He will open windows and pour out blessings. Your greatest punches come from staying low and remaining humble.

Father thank You for my lows. Thank You for my valleys. Without my lows I would not know how it feels to put complete trust in You. I pray that You continue to help me to grow and rise closer to You. From this day for forward, I will let the past be the past. No more looking back! I planted a seed, and I am strictly watering it and growing it from this point forward. In Jesus name, Amen.

Nothing Just Happens

"Wisdom is knowing the right path to take…Integrity is taking it"

-M.H. McKee-

Nothing in life just happens by chance. Do not underestimate God's plan for your life. God knows how to get us from A-Z. God isn't finished yet and He will bring to pass all that He has planned if we just remain humble, faithful, and hold on to His unchanging hand. You are anointed to be something, yet someone else holds the position.

Let's think of David and Goliath. God strategically placed Goliath there, but for David. Why? God knew what David would encounter, so it would bring out the best in him. To get to the next level in life, you must allow God to bring out the best in you.

Do not allow your gifts to lie still. There is something on the inside of you. As Christians, we must stay the course. We must hang in there and stay faithful to what God has ordained us to be. We must not get to ahead of ourselves, because God will take care of it one day at a time. God has already equipped us with everything we need to do what we are called to do.

It is only a test. The circumstances may be difficult but trusting God to use your circumstances will make you better and give you the ability to truly serve Him. Open your gifts and bring out what God has placed on the inside of you. Never allow someone who is in no position to do what you were positioned to do yourself. A writer once said, "Pictures aren't painted by the painter just pouring paint on a canvas, but it's one stroke at a time."

Lord, again I thank You. God, I pray that every distraction be eliminated and cast out so that I can see and be everything that You have called/ordained me to be. I pray that everything that is stopping me from my calling is put to rest. I pray that You continue to give me the strength to carry on, and the strength to continue to beat the odds. In Jesus name, Amen.

Happy New Year!!!

"Let the word of Christ dwell in your richly"

Colossians 3:16

As we enter a new year, we must remember there is no substitute for the time spent with our Father in heaven. As humans, we wait until the last minute to plan for the New Year. We wait until the first day of January to begin. We should never put off for tomorrow for what we can do today. Let's begin preparing today for our New Year. If you prolong, chances are you will never begin. Planning consist of prayer and meditation on the word of God, and how it will be significant in our lives. Without a plan, the most important things will always get pushed aside by urgent pressures.

If we want to be what God wants us to be, we must start now. We must be impactful, because tomorrow is not promised to us. Planning must be a regular part of your life. Procrastination is the killer for people who attempt to get to the next level but become frustrated and quit.

Our hearts and our characters will not change until our habits change. Time in God's word does not just happen. You must choose wisely to make it happen. *"Look carefully then how you walk, not as unwise but as wise, making the best use of the time, because the days are evil."* (Ephesians 5:15-16)

Dear Lord, thank You for making all things new. Thank You for all that You have allowed into our lives this past year, the good along with the hard things, which have reminded us how much we need You and rely on Your presence filling us every single day. I pray for Your Spirit to lead us each step of this New Year. I decree and declare that new blessings, new doors, and new beginnings will flow into our lives. Lord again, I thank You. In Jesus name, Amen.

Horizontal Work for a Vertical Word

"But I tell you that anyone who is angry with a brother or sister will be subject to judgement. Again, any who says to a brother or sister, 'Raca' is answerable to the court and anyone who says, 'You Fool' will be in danger of the fire of hell. Therefore, if you are offering your gift at the altar and there remember that your brother or sister has something against you, leave your gift there in front of the altar. First go and be reconciled to them; then come and offer your gift."

(Matthew 5:22-24)

How much soul saving are you offering? No matter where you go in this world, or in this season, you should offer salvation to each person you meet. Often, we bypass horizontal and go straight to vertical. God works with all types of relationships, but as Christian believers we must display a relationship with others just as we display a relationship with Christ. So many Christians get in church on Sunday morning and will shout but cannot speak to your brother or sister. When our motives are not pure, we will turn a deaf ear to worship. We receive nothing from God because we are not doing what God has asked us to do. We cannot move into worship until we fix our horizontal and then our vertical would be straight.

We tend to ask God for something, but then we are hard on everyone else. We spend time gossiping but stand still on Sunday morning during praise and worship. We want someone to deliver us, but we cannot deliver ourselves. There is so much sin in the church. As the songwriter once said, "Trying to love two isn't easy to do." We must prepare ourselves daily for hell and chaos. Below you will find three points on how to fix your horizontal:

• Grow up: Tricks are for kids, put away childish things and become mature in God

• Be humble and sit down: We go through because we will not let it go. We must humble ourselves and sit down. Allow God to work behind the scenes.

• Resolve Quickly: Do not wait to say I'm sorry or to resolve an issue, do it quickly, be mature enough to approach the individual.

Everyone needs grace and mercy. No one is perfect. We must allow ourselves to align up with God. We must practice what we speak. We can quote the bible, BUT are we living up to it? Are we applying it to our everyday life? Are we spending time in meditation with our creator? Are we giving Him our undivided attention? Loving two is hard to do. Will we love Him and obey His commandments? Will you make it into the kingdom? It is time to elevate your life, does your vertical align with your horizontal?

Lord, today I pray that You will allow me to be seated, and You speak for me. I pray that You allow me to humble myself and let You work within me. I pray that I will continue to grow more and more in You as the days go by. I thank You, I honor You, and I praise You. In Jesus name, Amen.

Your Lifeguard Walks on Water

"When you pass through the waters, I will be with you; and when you pass through the rivers, they will not sweep over you. When you walk through the fire, you will not be burned; the flames will not set you ablaze."

Isaiah 43:2

You may be going through a drowning situation where you just cannot seem to catch grip. Just hang in there, stay on top, and be faithful because the race is not given to the swift nor the battle to the strong, but to those who endured to the end.

Often, we try so hard to continue the race, yet we are spiritually drowning. You have reached your breaking point and you are worn out spiritually. You wake up and look in the mirror trying to encourage yourself but that can often seem impossible to do.

As Christians, we spend so much time active in church ministry, where you are always called to do something, yet you are drowning. You ask yourself what is wrong. We are in a season where it is hard to hold on. This is called a slippery slope. You see your life as a duck who is fighting a tough wave. Someone who is fighting hard to stay afloat, but remember your life guard walks on water.

Even at your lowest point in your life, God has the keys to your life and He can reach down and pull you up. The closer you get to God, the closer you are to walking on water too. Isaiah 40:31 reads, *"But those who hope in the LORD will renew their strength. They will soar on wings like eagles; they will run and not grow weary; the will walk and not be faint."*

To get to the next level you must walk on water, your lifeguard can and will teach you the impossible. *"Have I not commanded you? Be strong and courageous. Do not be afraid; do not be discourage, for the Lord your God will be with you wherever you do."* (Joshua 1:9)

Dear Lord, sometimes the day can't pass quickly enough. My heart is weary, and my spirit is weak. I am tired, Lord, but I am trying my hardest. Help me to remember the reason I began this race. Help me to see the purpose behind Your plan for my life. Keep me set upon Your face to find strength for the next step, and to discover faith to keep on trying. In Jesus name, Amen.

Broken Pieces Still Float

"Be strong and take heart, all your hope is in the Lord"

-Psalms 31:24

Paul was in a ship wreck. The ship tore into pieces and people were dying, but Paul's mindset was "We shall not die. We are going to make it." We will float on broken pieces, because broken pieces still float.

You may be living in a rough time and don't know what may come, but remember one thing, we are going to make it. "Trust in the Lord with all thine heart and lean not unto thy own understanding but in all ways, acknowledge Him and He shall direct your path. (Proverbs 3:5-6)

Life will not always be fair and there will come times where you will face many hardships and storms, but you must understand that God is so much bigger than what you may be facing. Jesus fed a multitude off two fish and five loaves of bread. They made it, and if Paul can do it so can you.

Paul made it happen. Paul made it off a broken ship, floating on broken pieces. Your life maybe in a shamble, but do not abandon the ship because broken pieces still float.

Dear Lord, although my life is rough right now, I thank You. Although the going gets tough, I thank you. Although situations and circumstances seem too hard to bare, I thank You. And most of all, I trust You. I believe that You will make a way out of no way. I believe that You will provide for me, and open doors that my little eyes cannot see. You will bring me out, alright. And for that Lord, I thank You. In Jesus name, Amen.

Your Storm Is for A Reason

You can't predict what life is going to throw at you. All you can do is ride through the storm and hope to see a rainbow on the other side.

-Nishan Panwar-

Aristotle once said, "As low as you might go is as high as you will fly. Your challenges can be a powerful energy source awakening you to rise higher than you might ever have gone." As we look in the mirror, we ask ourselves, "Why am I going through?" God only gives His toughest battles to His strongest soldiers. God has a motive behind everything He does. When we are going through our storm, here are two important things God wants us to know:

• God wants to show us that He can calm the storm---Peace be still

Even when we are going through the fire remember He is still there and He will bring you peace.

• God wants to calm you while you are going through your storm---Too often we become so high that we create our own storm and get mad when it begins to rain

When you become so high, you get to a place where no one can talk to you. There are people within your circle walking on eggshells. We cannot expect God to show us anyone else until He reveals who we really are. Our storms can be a distraction to take us off course or our storms can be motivation to calm us into being what and who God has created us to be. How will you predict your next storm? Will you let it calm you or will you allow it to destroy you.

God, again I thank You for every storm that has come our way. I pray that with every storm brings on a new lesson. I pray every storm that comes our way, is motivation. For we WILL BE everything that God has created us to be. In Jesus name, Amen.

I Have Purpose

"For we are God's workmanship, created in Christ Jesus to do good works, which God prepared in advanced for us to do."

Ephesians 2:10

Many people go through life feeling uncertain and discouraged about themselves and thinking that they have no purpose. When God calls you, it is for a purpose. God gives us purpose before we are born. He spiritually anointed us before our time. There are two things we should learn about life:

- You are not an accident---God Created YOU!

- You have purpose in life--- God has a plan for YOU!

Before God formed you in your mother's womb, He knew you and He set you apart from the rest. Our greatest anointing comes from our greatest struggles. If we never sin, we wouldn't be who we are. People's opinions do not stop the purpose God has for your life. People will judge you off what they see. There are so many things in life that will cause us to turn away from our true purpose, such as, smoking, drinking, gambling, and fornication. We will continue to go in circles. No matter how we try to hide, or where we try to run, the call and the purpose on our life will always remain.

One purpose in this life is to glorify God, praise, and worship Him. Psalm 86:12 reads, *"I will praise you, O Lord my God, with all my heart; I will glorify your name forever."* We are created to grow in the spirit of God and spread His word to lost souls. We must walk into our purpose. Every living creature has a purpose. A writer name William Craig once wrote, *"You must have purpose imposed from the outside and God is needed to impose those purposes on it from the inside."*

Father, I know You have a plan for each of our lives, and I understand that the desire for every one of Your children is to know You more and more and to live our life in a manner that is pleasing to You. Help me to face the challenges of life by looking to Jesus and relying on His sufficient strength and grace. Help me not to repay evil for evil, but to love my enemies and to do good to those that spitefully use me. In Jesus name, Amen.

Let Go and Forgive

"Bear with each other and forgive whatever grievance you may have against one another. Forgive as the Lord has forgiven you."

Colossians 3:13

Forgiveness is a choice we make through our decision of our own will, motivated by obedience to our Savior. The act of forgiveness does not come easy for many us as Christians. No matter how bad you are treated, you must learn to forgive and let go. Even if you are in the wrong, it is still best to forgive so our God in heaven can forgive us.

It may hurt, but we have many things on the inside that we need God to forgive us for. Therefore, as believers we must forgive to get to the promise land. If you asked yourself these questions you will come up with various answers:

• Have you been lied on? Typically, the answer would be YES.

•	Have you lied on someone? Again, a typical answer would be YES.

How can we expect God to open Heaven and pour out blessings if we can't forgive our brothers and sisters? How can we throw a rock and hide our hands? God said, *"Let he who is without sin cast the first stone."* As Christian believers, we must forgive by faith and out of obedience. God honors us when we show commitment and obey His will. Author Lewis Smedes wrote, *"When you release the wrongdoer from the wrong, you cut a malignant tumor out your inner life. You set a prisoner free, but you discover that the real prisoner was yourself."* We must forgive those who have hurt us so we can live free in the promise land.

Dear Lord, thank You for the gift of forgiveness. Your only Son loved me enough to come to earth and experience the worst pain imaginable, so I could be forgiven. Your mercy flows to me in spite of my faults and failures. Help me to demonstrate unconditional love, even to those who have hurt me. Help me to release the hurt and begin to love as Jesus loves. If I can be forgiven, so can I forgive. In Jesus name, Amen.

Straighten It Out

"Consider the work of God, for who can straighten what he hath crooked?"

Ecclesiastes 7:13

Gospel singer Shirley Caesar once said, "Though pressures of life seem to weigh you down, although sometimes you have to walk alone, and now you are asking yourself is there a word from the Lord. You need a blessing and you need it right away. God is concerned, and He is working out for you."

In our life, we will fall, we shall stumble, and we will doubt God. As mentioned before, you are going to walk, and you will not hear God's voice. God is behind the scenes working it out in our favor. God has covered you from everything that was meant to break you.

In sickness, tribulation, on the job issues, broken marriages, troubled teens, betrayal from family members, unfaithful leaders in the church and angry co-workers. You are the point of no return. You have cried, prayed, and it seems like you are getting nowhere. {You must remember, God has already straightened it out} You shall live and not die. Everything that is asked in the name of Jesus is already done.

Promotion is already done. Healing is already done. Broken marriages, God has already straightened it out. Financial increase, it is already done, and broken hearts are already healed in the name of Jesus.

God did not design us to give up. He created us to lean not unto our own understanding but in all ways, acknowledge Him and He shall direct our path. If we place our burden at His feet and leave it there, we must know He will deliver.

As Christians, and as believers, we must trust His plan for our lives. God will not place more on us than we can bear. Chains are being broken, and shackles are coming off, because we serve a most high God. A blues singer once wrote a song entitled, "Let's straighten it out." In this song, he wanted to straighten out issues he had with his significant other. Today let us allow God to work behind the scenes on our behalf. We must allow God to work things out even when we ourselves do not see a way. As believers of Christ, let us establish a true relationship with God and solely trust His plan for our lives.

Lord, I just want to thank You. You have assigned me my portion and my cup; You have my lot secure. You have made known to me the path and plan of my life; You will fill me with joy in Your presence, and with eternal pleasures at Your right hand. I have nothing to fear with You on my side. In Jesus name, Amen.

Only A Matter of Time

"There will come a point in your life when you've had enough, and you must let go of things that keep weighing you down. You must understand no matter how convincing they seem, that you can't do without them, it's just a matter of time that you will get over it."

-Author Unknown-

God had you here for a specific time, because He knows where you are in life. God will not move you until He is ready to place you where He wants you to be. Often, we want to be blessed because others around us are being blessed, but God said, "It is not your time." We must learn to be humble and allow God to move when we are mature enough to accept the blessings being brought forth. God is requiring us to grow up. We want a mature blessing, yet we are still immature in our ways. If you are wondering why you are not being blessed in a timely manner, here is the reason:

- It is not your time.

- God is waiting on you to disconnect yourself from the wrong people.

- I do not know (His way is not our way).

Do not expect blessings if you are still attached to the wrong people. You cannot have moved forth in life if you are surrounded by negativity and drama. You must disconnect yourself. Where God is trying to take you, there is no room for drama. Your time is limited. You are blessed by association. As Christian believers, we must learn to disconnect ourselves. When you do so, it does not mean that you are "acting funny." It simply means that the person you were connected to did not give to your life. You must connect with people who are moving forward in Christ, and who are believers of His word. When you connect with the right people, everyone who is attached to your WINS.

Father, I thank You for blessing me with the ability to choose my friends and the people I chose to associate with wisely. I refuse to surround myself with undisciplined, uncontrolled, and irresponsible people who will pull me down their wayward ways. I trust that the Godly characteristics I see in their lives will rub off on me, and I will become better for it. I surround myself with the right people, I hear the right things, I receive the right influences, and I am becoming the right person. The one You desire me to be. I declare this by faith! In Jesus name, Amen.

Passages to Help You Get to the Next Level Spiritually

Though he slays me, yet will I trust in him: but I will maintain mine own ways before him. (Job 13:15)

Finally, brothers and sisters, whatever is true, whatever is noble, whatever is right, whatever is pure, whatever is lovely, whatever is admirable--if anything is excellent or praiseworthy--think about such things. (Phil 4:8)

Let the words of my mouth, and the meditation of my heart, be acceptable in thy sight, O LORD, my strength, and my redeemer. (Psalm 19:14)

Keep thy heart with all diligence; for out of it are the issues of life. (Proverbs 4:23)

Brethren, I do not regard myself as having laid hold of it yet; but one thing I do: forgetting what lies behind and reaching forward to what lies ahead, I press on toward the goal for the prize of the upward call of God in Christ Jesus (Phil 3:13-14)

Because of this, I always try to maintain a clear conscience before God and all people. (Acts 24:16)

We destroy every proud obstacle that keeps people from knowing God. We capture their rebellious thoughts and teach them to obey Christ. (2 Corinthians 10:5)

Create in me a clean heart, O God, and renew a steadfast spirit within me. (Psalms 51:10)

"Do not be overcome by evil, but overcome evil with good" (Romans 12:21).

"Are not five sparrows sold for two pennies? Yet not one of them is forgotten by God. Indeed, the very hairs of your head are all numbered. Don't be afraid; you are worth more than many sparrows" (Luke 12:6-7).

"And when you stand praying, if you hold anything against anyone, forgive them, so that your Father in heaven may forgive you your sins" (Mark 11:25).

"Therefore, since we are receiving a kingdom that cannot be shaken, let us be thankful, and so worship God acceptably with reverence and awe, for our "God is a consuming fire" (Hebrews 12:28-29).

"We want each of you to show this same diligence to the very end, so that what you hope for may be fully realized" (Hebrews 6:11).

"Since, then, you have been raised with Christ, set your hearts on things above, where Christ is, seated at the right hand of God" (Colossians 3:1).

For to this you have been called, because Christ also suffered for you, leaving you an example, so that you might follow in his steps. He committed no sin, neither was deceit found in his mouth. When he was reviled, he did not revile in return; when he suffered, he did not threaten, but continued entrusting himself to him who judges justly. He himself bore our sins in his body on the tree, that we might die to sin and live to righteousness. By his wounds, you have been healed. {1 Peter 2:21-24}

10 Keys to Help You Get to the Next Level in Life

- Accept Your Calling

- Look for Confirmation

- Allow your past to be a blessing for your future

- Accept change

- Commit yourself to God

- Build a relationship with God

- Be prepared for spiritual attacks

- Accept who God has ordained you to be

- Remember change is a process

- Walk By faith and Not by Sight

Journal Pages

Made in the USA
Columbia, SC
25 November 2024

46939949R00054